SIMPLE SHORTCUTS
TO WINNING AT LIFE

*Simple and effective instructions
on how to become
the master of your life*

NAOMI STOCKMAN

BALBOA.
PRESS

A DIVISION OF HAY HOUSE

Balboa Press books may be ordered through booksellers or by contacting:

Balboa Press
A Division of Hay House
1663 Liberty Drive
Bloomington, IN 47403
www.balboapress.com
1 (877) 407-4847

Because of the dynamic nature of the Internet, any web addresses or links contained in this book may have changed since publication and may no longer be valid. The views expressed in this work are solely those of the author and do not necessarily reflect the views of the publisher, and the publisher hereby disclaims any responsibility for them.

The author of this book does not dispense medical advice or prescribe the use of any technique as a form of treatment for physical, emotional, or medical problems without the advice of a physician, either directly or indirectly. The intent of the author is only to offer information of a general nature to help you in your quest for emotional and spiritual well-being. In the event you use any of the information in this book for yourself, which is your constitutional right, the author and the publisher assume no responsibility for your actions.

Any people depicted in stock imagery provided by Thinkstock are models, and such images are being used for illustrative purposes only.
Certain stock imagery © Thinkstock.

Print information available on the last page.

ISBN: 978-1-5043-0181-7 (sc)
ISBN: 978-1-5043-0182-4 (e)

Balboa Press rev. date: 05/03/2016

FOREWORD

The principles in this book can be applied in any area of your life. If you have a particular thing you want to change or develop, you can focus just on this area, for example, your business, your health, or your relationship. The more you focus and perform the exercises, the better the results you will experience.

CONTENTS

MY STORY

I guess the only way to explain my situational life at the age of twenty one is to say that I had let life happen to me without practicing any deliberate directional influence on the outcomes.

It never occurred to me during the transition from child to adult that a person's life was the result of strategic choices, but rather I accepted the actions and choices of other people, and just went along with whatever was happening on any given day and any given time. So effectively, I had remained a child in that respect - just dealing with whatever was dealt to me, like a leaf being swept down a rainy gutter.

I left home at fifteen with a boy I had met twice. Not as a deliberate choice, but swept up by a series of events that landed me on his white haired, petite, elderly grandmother's couch, and as no one made me go home, I never did. Having just completed year nine of high school, I began working days as a supermarket cashier, and nights as a waitress, which gave me something I had never had before - money - and that marked the end of my high schooling.

Within a few months of leaving home, another series of events took the pair of us to a remote town in far North Queensland where, like two vagrant child nomads, we worked the fields with aboriginal men, mowed lawns, picked fruit, and worked in kitchens. Neither of us had a birth certificate, bank account, or any identification. Realistically, we could have disappeared from the face of the earth and no one would ever have noticed.

There were nine pubs in this one-horse town. Half the population were native, and drinking was the primary pastime. Segregation between the whites and aboriginals was subtle, but present, and one pub was known to be 'the black pub' where all the darkies congregated, and white people didn't enter. Local stories included all kinds of drunken tales of shotgun fire and crazy antics, and my observation was that alcohol was definitely a significant social problem.

I had my sixteenth birthday living upstairs in that pub. Two white kids in a room with two single beds - it was all we could afford, and thankfully we were safe. I can only begin to imagine the horrendous worry my mother endured not knowing where I was or if I was safe.

I could write a whole book on just this six month period of my life. Overall it was a happy time full of adventure, incredible experiences, interesting people, and best of all - freedom! But let's continue.

We moved back to Sydney by the end of that year and, after completing a short course, I became a receptionist in a large corporate organisation in Sydney CBD. I was now associating with young professionals, making new friends, and feeling driven! My goals were being formed, I was learning a lot and earning a lot. I felt excited about life... for a short time.

Like any children, as we grew up, we changed. I became more sensible, he became more reckless. I quit smoking, he took up hard drugs. I got a good job, he took up crime. Life spiralled downward into a chaotic mess and ironically as we grew further apart it became harder and harder to part ways, but inevitably by twenty one I was alone and broke, with two young children aged one and four.

There are always choices in the face of adversity - lay down and give up, or fight like hell - and I was a fighter. There was no way I was going to continue in the life I had put myself in. I felt like a stranger, trapped in someone else's reality. The people around me were nothing like me. I felt so alien and so far from where I belonged with no clue what to do. One day I picked up a card on the ground - on that card were the words "CHOICE NOT CHANCE DETERMINE YOUR DESTINY"... Up until that moment, I had been living my life by chance, not choice. That card and the resulting realisation changed my life forever.

I'd like to say from that moment on I was amazing - that I made perfect choices - found the man of my dreams - raised two perfect kids - and became a beacon of inspiration. But that's far from the case. I did begin learning about the power of the mind and read many self-help books by well reputed authors. I did form goals and apply many of the success techniques that I still use today, but like many people, my goals were unbalanced. I refer to the next period of my life as a period of transition, where I tipped like a giant see-saw from uneducated and poor, to educated and wealthy, while neglecting every other aspect of my life, my soul, and my happiness. Half way into this transition phase my life literally fell apart. I left my clinically functional relationship based on common ambition, became chronically ill with lung infections, developed cancer, and had a tremendous breakdown. I was twenty nine, and my children, now twelve and nine were terrified.

Again, I'd like to say I had an epiphany, and indeed in some aspect I probably did, but the only thing I can say about the next seven years following my cancer treatment was I clearly hadn't learned my lesson yet. I went right back to my functional, ambition based relationship, entered the world of business and had a third child. I've read somewhere that people either move towards pleasure, or away from pain – whichever influence is the most powerful, and for me at that time, being alone was my greatest fear, so I filled my house with as many people as possible. Life was so busy I could barely notice my unhappiness. I had my two kids, a new baby, a foster child, my friend's mother, and a husband who contributed very little in the way of daily support, all living in my one enormous house, in addition to a business with sixteen staff to run. I was now in my thirties and heading for another proverbial brick wall at high speed.

The brick wall came in the form of an overseas employee. A faceless voice on the phone, who spoke to me for many hours about his life, his loves, his family, his friends, his childhood, his thoughts and his feelings. It was like oxygen to my deprived soul and the realisation of just how unhappy I truly was crashed my world like a house of cards. My husband believed I was leaving him for this man. But the truth was, I just couldn't live the rest of my life like that, without purpose or fulfilment. I knew if I didn't do something to change my life and create the life I wanted, I would die with regret.

The next few years were challenging. I focused hard on myself and changed a lot. On the morning of writing this I listened to an audio book that aptly explained the necessity of struggle during a growth transition using a caterpillar fighting its way out of the cocoon as an example. It is by adversity that we grow and transform ourselves for the better. During those years I travelled to three developing countries alone, bought a kayak, and through nothing short of a miracle, bought three houses, in spite of the fact that I had re-started my life with very little money. Looking back, now, it's almost like every person I needed was brought to me at exactly the right moment, and many left again as I moved on to another stage in my transition.

I want to interject here with a very important fact: - Every single person that is brought into our lives is there for a reason, a season, or a lifetime... and though we tend to make 'attachments', the secret to success is to remain fluid and accepting as people come and go from our lives. People often mistake attachment for love. Love is a powerful energy that elevates us and those around us, attachment is a fear based energy that stops us from moving forward and holds us back. In fact, letting go is one of the essential disciplines required for success which I will share with you in the following chapters.

So let me tell you where my life is at now, and then I will step out the essential disciplines that you can apply to have, do and be anything you can imagine and have the happiness and success you desire and deserve in your life.

Right now,

I look and feel younger than I did five years ago.
I am twice as wealthy after losing everything five years ago than I was before.
I work half as much as I did five years ago.
I have twice as much income as I did five years ago.
I laugh, smile and play twice as much as I did five years ago.
I have twice as much energy as I did five years ago.
I have the kind of relationship I always wanted, with the type of man I always dreamed of.
I have a great job with people I love.
I am preparing to launch a great business.
I have published a book.

Every day I wake up happy and enthusiastic about my life. Fear, guilt, anger and sadness are no longer things I frequently experience.
I have confidence and I feel great about myself, and as my life changes in the years to come I know I will be equipped to embrace the opportunities and overcome the obstacles.

The promise I make to you is that if you follow the disciplines of happiness and success I am going to share with you in the following chapters, you too can have the joy of living a wonderful life of complete abundance.

INTRODUCTION

What I am going to share with you works 100%, without fail, every time. I have countless mind boggling examples I can give you from my own life, and once you know how it works, you will see that it works exactly for every person you know, in their current life and circumstances.

It is simple, but it isn't easy - like the saying goes, the best things in life are simple to learn, but difficult to master. This is exactly true for self-mastery.

Using these techniques you will be able to:

- Move from poverty to unlimited wealth.
- Move from being bullied and rejected, to being empowered and accepted.
- Move from overweight, to slim, fit, healthy, sexy and attractive.
- Move from a low income, to a high income.
- Move from a mundane job, to a job you love.
- Move from loneliness, to companionship.
- Move from unloved, to loved and adored.
- Move from exhaustion, to vitality.
- Move from depression, to happiness.
- Move from anxious and stressed, to confident and relaxed.
- Move from average, to EXCEPTIONAL!

The most astounding thing we can realise about life is, we are only limited by our own beliefs.

Say that to yourself now. "I am only limited by my OWN BELIEFS" Once you truly realise this you have opened the door to your **unlimited potential**.

The beliefs that have stopped you from already having all the things you desire are called "Limiting Beliefs". In a later chapter we will look at how to:

1. Identify limiting beliefs

2. Challenge limiting beliefs

3. Analyse what will happen if we keep the limiting beliefs

4. Replace limiting beliefs with EMPOWERING beliefs

CHAPTER 1

THE SCIENCE OF THE MIND

You can change your reality if you are willing to adapt your perception and explore viewing life from different angles.

The difference between you, and any other person (aside from your physical attributes) is your mind.

If you take two people, similar height, weight, origin of birth, one may grow up to be confident, wealthy, fit, healthy, have many friends, a great job, happy family, travel and live an expanded, exceptional life inspiring those around them. The other person, in spite of having no visible disadvantage, may grow up to struggle, have poor health, bad luck and misfortune.

I have personally observed, spoken to, and analysed the difference between those people that fall into the first category, and those people that fall into the second category. Here are the differences in summary:

1. HOW CAN I SOLVE THIS Vs WHY DID THIS HAPPEN TO ME - AND WHO CAN I BLAME

When presented with adversity, a successful person will not dwell on the problem. They will assess the facts, and compose a strategy of action to rectify the problem and then prevent recurrence. Even if the problem was caused by an external party, they will seek an optimum outcome and not waste energy on being vengeful.

An unsuccessful person will dwell in the emotional frustration of the situation and waste energy blaming others and plotting revenge. Even if the actions of others are the cause of a problem, wasting energy blaming is destructive, not constructive.

2. WHAT CAN I DO TO HELP MYSELF, Vs WHY ISN'T SOMEONE HELPING ME

A successful person will focus on what they can do to move towards a goal. They will identify what options are available to them, and then begin taking action.

An unsuccessful person will focus on the problem, and when thinking of solutions will feel as though other people that could help them have let them down.

3. I CAN IF I, Vs I CAN'T BECAUSE

A successful person will think how they CAN do something. If they can't do something, they will think of how they could do it. For example, "If I study at night, I can get a better job" or "If I work a second job on Saturdays, I can save up for a house"

An unsuccessful person will tell you why they can't. For example, "I can't get a better job because I've already tried" or "I can't buy a house because I don't earn enough"

4. HOW CAN I MAKE MY FUTURE BETTER, Vs HOW CAN I GET WHAT I WANT RIGHT NOW

A successful person will sacrifice their efforts now, to have something in the future. For example, a successful person will live in a small cheap unit and drive an old car to save for a house in the future.

An unsuccessful person will want everything now. For example, an unsuccessful person will rent a nice house and borrow money for a nice car then say they can't save for a house.

5. PERSEVERE AND ADAPT Vs FRUSTRATION AND FAILURE

A successful person knows success is possible if they take the right actions and will keep trying different things until they get the result they want. They ask themselves, 'what can I do differently?'

An unsuccessful person tries one approach over and over, like hitting their head against a brick wall, and when that doesn't work, they tell everyone how hard they tried, saying 'look at the bruises to prove it' then they give up. They ask themselves 'why doesn't anything I try ever work?'

Successful people know that if someone else has achieved something, then they too can achieve it. They believe in their own ability and are prepared to learn from their mistakes. Even if something doesn't turn out, or they fail at an attempt, they will not be deterred or worried, but continue moving towards their goals in one way or another. They are not shy to ask for help, or to learn from the knowledge of others. They are able to work with others and maintain relationships with people for mutual gain.

HOW JUDGING AFFECTS YOU

When you pass critical judgement on something or someone outside of yourself, you are actually causing your perceptual box to shrink. You are literally binding yourself with the net that you cast onto others. Critical Judgement is different to Discerning Judgement.

Discerning Judgement is where you make a choice that applies to you. For example, I choose to dress well and keep my car clean because I want to be a clean, respectable person. Discerning Judgement is about what you will and won't accept in relation to you. Discerning Judgement is important, because it is how we choose who we want to be, and who we want to spend our time with. It is how we choose where to live, and what we eat. Discerning Judgement is about us and our own life.

Critical Judgement relates to applying your Discerning Judgement upon someone else who does not fit your choices. For example "Look at that filthy grub in those dirty clothes getting into that beat up car, clearly he is a loser".

The issue with Critical Judgment is it actually damages you. The neurological path you are building in order to condemn others is one that acts like cement in your mind, disallowing flexible thought and binding you to a narrow perception. This restricts you from thinking freely and objectively. You can see this clearly in older people who have been practicing for many decades... they are unable to appreciate concepts that do not fit into their current mould, and therefore cannot accept changes in society.

In addition, Critical Judgements come from a closed mind stuck in a single view perception. Critical Judgement is like a set of scales that measures every worth by the same scale without accounting for differences in material or circumstance. For example, a litre of petrol is completely different to a litre of milk, regardless of how they are packaged, and no amount of judgement will qualify one to become the other. Similarly, the grubby person with the dirty old car may in fact be a wealthy farmer.

The truth is, Critical Judgement is about rejecting someone as being less than you are. Focus upwards; look up for inspiration and aspiration, not downwards with condemnation and judgement. See the good in people no matter how challenged their exterior.

Adopt the belief that each and every person is doing the best they can with what they have right now – Because remember, no one can be any more or any less than what they think they are. People need our understanding, not our judgement. Adopting this mind set will set you free to accelerate your own success.

BIOLOGICAL FACTS

It is a fact that our brains are made up of neurons (cells), and the 'map' of our neurons is created by our experiences. As we grow up, our brain is programmed by learning from our parents, our teachers, our peers and the things that happen around us, and to us. We develop our values, our beliefs and create strategies for almost everything. If we are early risers, it is because we have developed a strategy for getting up early, if we are late sleepers, it is because we have not developed a strategy for getting up early. We think we are seeing life as it really is, but all we are doing is INTERPRETING the world according to the programming we received through our upbringing.

It is commonly accepted as fact that in each second we are exposed to two million bits of information and our meagre brains can only process one hundred and thirty two bits per second - so really, the way you interpret the world depends on you, and which one hundred and thirty two bits you pick up and process in each second. Narrow minded people assume that what they think and interpret as reality is 'right' - more intelligent people understand the limitations of the human mind and realise that 'reality' as we know it, is defined by the individual, therefore, each person's reality is different. The ability to accept that a person's reality varies depending on perception, and develop a genuine curiosity for learning other people's realities is the beginning of 'self-awareness'.

Every person truly believes the way they perceive the world and the way they think is right. It is this limitation within us that keeps us trapped and causes conflict between people.

You can change your reality if you are willing to adapt your perception and explore viewing life from different angles. The more restricted a person's perception, the more 'narrow minded' they are. Broad minded people are able to solve problems more easily, think more laterally, identify opportunities in situations and accept change more easily.

Successful people frequently venture outside of their comfort zone and expose themselves to people, activities and situations that are different from their own norm. Variety is important for a flexible mind.

CHAPTER 2

LIFE AS YOU KNOW IT

First you must know where you are, and then you must know where you want to go. Those are the first two steps in achieving anything.

So, let's get started!

Step one in the process of getting from where ever you are now, to where you want to be is to do a 'stock take' of exactly where you are now.

Because our lives are made up of various different areas, and usually some require more work than others, we need to take stock of each one individually.

Take a notebook, and at the top of 8 pages write the following headings:

HOME LIFE AND FAMILY

HEALTH AND FITNESS

FRIENDSHIPS AND SOCIAL LIFE

LOVE AND ROMANCE

FINANCES

WORK AND CAREER

PERSONAL DEVELOPMENT/ACHIEVEMENT

ENVIRONMENT

Next to the heading write a score out of 10 for how happy you are in that area of your life. For example, if you are super content with your home life and family, put 10/10 next to the heading on that page.

If you are extremely unhappy with your health and fitness, put 1/10 next to the heading on that page.

Remember, 10/10 is your absolute ideal!

Once you have done that, draw a horizontal line to divide the page in half and in the top half write in bullet point form all the things you want in that area of your life, regardless of whether you have it already or not. Put every detail of what you want for a perfect score.

Then under the line, write in present tense - "I am" "I have" "I can" - the correlating statement of your perfect score. Be as specific as you can. For example, rather than putting 'lose weight' define the exact weight you would like to be. Rather than saying 'have more money' define exactly the amount you would like to have. See the example on health and fitness below.

HEALTH AND FITNESS   4/10

Weigh 60kg

Comfortably fit size 10 clothing

Exercise 2 times a week with friends

Able to run 5km without stopping

Enjoy healthy foods

Drink plenty of water

Feel good about my body

Feel attractive and look nice

Have a firm flat stomach

I am slim, fit, healthy, sexy and attractive. I comfortably slide into my size 10 jeans and I feel great about my body. I know I look good and I feel attractive. Every day, I enjoy healthy foods, fruits, vegetables, natural foods and I drink plenty of fresh clean water. I enjoy running and I easily run further and further each week. Running 5 kilometres is easy and enjoyable and I am inspired when I see how fit I am. My body is becoming firmer and leaner as I enjoy my healthy fresh food and exercise. I have friends who enjoy exercising with me and I am happy and encouraged. I am strong and firm and I feel fantastic when I stand on the scales and see the 60.00 kg on the dial. This is the true me.

Do this for every heading. It's also beneficial to include time frames, for example, I'm so excited at the 30th of June to see the $250,000 in my bank account.

By the end of this exercise you will have 8 pages with passionate statements of your perfect life, written as though you already have it all. We will go back to this later when we discuss 'Daily Talk'.

Every person's life can be likened to a box where the walls are their fears and limitations. Some people's box is very small, and other people's box is bigger. Everything you currently have in your life, is inside your box, and everything you want, that you don't have yet, is outside your box, outside your limiting beliefs and your walls of fear. The walls are there to satisfy your biological need for safety. After food, shelter, clothing (physiological needs) safety is the next highest priority in your self-preservation.

By creating a clear and written 10/10 goal set for every area of your life, you have the first step of achieving anything, and that is the clarity to know what it is you actually want. This needs to be reinforced over and over in your mind.

These things described in your 'ideals' may be things you don't already have. This means they are currently 'outside your box'. Therefore you will need to make changes to gain these things as realities in your life. The most important thing we need to change to change our life, and reality, is our MIND. We can resize that 'box' to include new and exciting things for our future to become one that we choose and design with deliberation.

CHAPTER 3

CREATE THE DREAM

You can have, do and be ANYTHING your mind can image... So start imagining!

Whatever the mind can CONCEIVE and BELIEVE - the mind can ACHIEVE! *Napoleon Hill.*

When speaking with people who have already achieved success, one of the notable traits they have is that they have very clear plans for the future. These plans are specific, detailed, and often documented. They can see it in their mind. They know exactly what it will feel like when they have it, and they have certainty that they will achieve their plans.

With a crystal clear picture of what you want, your subconscious mind (the part of your mind that determines which 132 bits of information to process out of the 2 million each second) will have a destination to move towards, and your life will gain purposeful direction. The more detail you can add to your goal, the better. People who don't know exactly what they want, seldom get it - how can they? The mind has to conceive and believe to achieve!

And trust me, WHATEVER you believe, you will achieve. If you believe 'life is a struggle', that's what you'll get. If you believe 'All men/women are cheats and liars', that's what you'll get. If you believe everyone is an idiot, you will see nothing but the idiocy of each person you meet.

Every person's life is a reflection of what is within them. Change what is within and your external life will change too. Change the way you think, your attitude, your beliefs and your habits to match those of someone who already has what you want, and you will be on the way to achieving your dreams.

When we worry about things, we create a clear picture of a negative outcome. We see it in our mind, feel it with our emotions, and focus on it. We believe that we are in imminent danger and our emotions come as though this potential fear is already happening. This is a sure way to attract the things we DON'T want in our lives.

Worry is low level anxiety caused by fear of something that will probably never happen. Worry is the opposite of faith, and faith is essential to success. Worry is like rust, corroding your soul. Kill it, replace it, and train your faith to be stronger than your fear. Successful people are fearless. Successful leaders are fearless. To achieve anything, you need to be able to take fearless action. Fear is a crippling disease that keeps people exactly where they are, and if you can't progress, you can't succeed.

A well-known theory about human behaviour is that there are only two basic emotions that drive us, Fear and Love, and every action of every person is rooted in one or the other. It is simple to say "Don't be afraid" - but managing emotional responses is a skill which requires practice. First you must be aware that the hurt, anger, frustration, jealousy, insecurity or whatever destructive feeling you have is caused by some kind of fear... then identify exactly what thoughts have triggered this fear, and REPLACE THE THOUGHTS. Logically, it would make sense to say that if all behavior is rooted in fear or love – then the antidote for any negative emotion or behavior is LOVE. One technique I use to replace thoughts is questioning myself, ask questions to bring the fear into perspective. Another is to begin focusing on GRATITUDE (gratitude uses the opposite part of the brain to fear and cannot operate simultaneously). And lastly is to practice and really focus on manifesting techniques.

MANIFESTING 101

Every self-help guru from here to Tibet will testify to the power of 'manifesting', and it works!

Let me tell you just a few examples from my own life.

I was twenty three and broke. For me at that time, money was my biggest problem. So I created a vision - to be worth two hundred and fifty thousand dollars. This was the biggest amount my mind could fathom at that time and seemed as impossible as landing on the moon to someone that could barely afford basic living. I applied every one of the principles of manifestation with dedicated passion. I didn't rob banks, I didn't sell drugs, I just used the manifestation techniques and went about my life. Exactly five years later I went through a legal separation with my then husband and on the asset sheet my half of the assets were exactly two hundred and fifty thousand dollars. When I met him he was a second year apprentice with a car loan and not a cent in the bank. We had acquired half a million dollars in five years. This is not a coincidence. I manifested my vision.

When I was studying accounting, I decided I wanted to be a TAFE teacher. I said "In five years I will teach accounting at TAFE" I could see it clearly in my mind - Exactly five years later, I was offered an opportunity by a fellow university student, who happened to be the head teacher of the accounting faculty at TAFE. I walked off the street and into a classroom and taught for seven years. This is not a coincidence.

Have you ever met someone who just tries and tries and gets nowhere? It's like at every corner they hit a road block. Their life is like a series of unfortunate events, bad luck, and missed opportunities.

These people are applying the exact same principles for achieving success, but in reverse. They are manifesting failure instead of success.

OWNING YOUR LIFE

Your whole life is a result of what you think. Your life is a result of your beliefs and your values.

The one most important belief that you must hold true in your mind to succeed is this:

I AM RESPONSIBLE FOR EVERYTHING IN MY LIFE.

This is critical.

And that means EVERYTHING.

There is NOTHING in your life that you have not attracted or manifested yourself.

Even the people you meet. The 'accidents'. The stuff that's unfair. The sicknesses.

Some people want to argue this - saying "what about the innocent children who don't ask to be beaten, or sick, or poor" - I don't have the answer, and I don't care to debate. I'm just telling you the facts that I have found to be true through observation, and the study of successful people. To succeed, you have to be willing to say: "What about ME has caused this and how can I improve it?" The more self-accountable a person is, the more successful they will be. Blaming outside factors will sink you.

People love to take credit for their successes "I got to this point in my career through my own hard work and dedication" and then judge others for their short falls. This kind of ego gloating will stall you from achieving the next level of success. Any time you are looking outside yourself with judgement or blame, you are detracting from your positive flow and reducing your own success. No matter what someone else does, refrain from judging and refrain from blaming. After all, there is always someone smarter and more successful than you that may view your victories as pathetic compared to theirs. Truly successful people are too busy looking upwards to put others down. Stay in the position of Self Accountability - Focus on moving forward and always be benevolent and kind, no matter what someone else does. Every negative energy you have, will be like a snag holding you back from flowing forward.

CREATING THE FUTURE "YOU"

We often see our lives from within ourselves, looking out. So our planning, and our desires, are largely focused on the things around us. Our home, our work, our car, our friends, our finances, our family etc. are all outside of us. I had been using manifesting in some way or another for approximately twenty years on and off when I sought help from an NLP (Neuro Linguistic Programming) professional. It was through him that I realised, that I had invested my focus on changing my life from the outside in. Yes, I had improved many things about myself and my life, but I hadn't created the ideal 'me'. Because of this, there was an ever present gut wrenching fear that I wasn't good enough and wasn't worthwhile. It felt like it was eating at me that none of the things I tried seemed to shift.

He gave me the task to create in my mind a detailed version of the ideal me. How I look, how I feel, my clothes, my disposition - every detail of the perfectly calm, perfectly happy, perfectly confident and assured, perfectly created ME. He told me to spend a few minutes, six times a day, visualising this 'ideal me'. Perhaps smiling, in a nice setting, and just focusing on the love and acceptance I feel for myself.

The logic behind this, is it slowly programs your subconscious to accept the created future you. If the current version of you isn't in alignment with version of you that your subconscious has accepted, then your subconscious will action the changes needed for you to become the person you have designed. This may mean a reduction in weight, change in disposition, change in situation, or whatever you have created for yourself.

We can never be anything more or less, than we see ourselves as, and our subconscious believes we are. If we have deep insecurities, fears and doubts about ourselves, our worth, our situations, these will stop us from having all the joy and happiness we deserve, and cause us loss and pain.

CHAPTER 4

DAILY THANK

No matter what your circumstance, when you shift your focus away from the things you don't have, and feel thankful for the things you do have, you are on the way to receiving miracles.

There is a universal relationship between happiness and gratefulness and an inverse parallel between complaining, and unhappiness.

Every thought we have, affects the way we feel. Every feeling we experience, attracts more of that feeling.

Many people focus on 'lack.

Even the concept of 'wanting' is focusing on lack.

When we 'want' the feeling is that of 'not having' something.

This is why it is so important when visualising and chanting for manifestation, that we speak in the present tense as though we already HAVE what we desire. See it, feel it... thank for it.

And each day, thank for as many things as possible. The feeling of being lucky, blessed, and having plenty, will attract more of that feeling. No matter how tragic things may seem, if you shift your focus from that of tragedy, to one of being blessed, you are on the way to receiving miracles.

Every religion in the world agrees on the principle of thankfulness.

Every religion in the world agrees on faith.

Every religion in the world agrees on prayer.

The basic system supported by every religion is "thank, ask, thank, believe, thank, receive, and thank again"

Ask, believe, receive - and be grateful.

Did you know that it is impossible to be grateful and fearful at the same time? It uses two opposite parts of the brain, so if you are worrying about something... start thanking... and the part of your brain that is worrying will be disabled.

CHAPTER 5

DAILY THINK

Your thoughts are like wind in the sails of your ship of destiny. Your future lies in the precise direction of your thoughts. Think with purpose!

The brain is like any other aspect of your being. It improves with training and repetition. This is true for the way you think.

You can now understand that what you think determines what you say, how you feel, who you are and ultimately, what you do.

It is very important to make sure you are always thinking as though you are in the driver's seat of your life.

Nothing in your life is ever anyone else's fault. You are the driver of your own life. The creator of your own destiny. No one can live your life but you.

Whenever we BLAME anything outside of ourselves we are giving away our power.

Whenever we BLAME anyone or anything outside of ourselves we are allowing ourselves to be a victim.

A victim is not a winner. A victim is not empowered. When you blame, you give away your power and render yourself mentally helpless.

Let me remind you of my story. I was twenty years old. I had two children. I was uneducated and unemployed. The father of my children was a drug addict. He was often psychotic, violent and unpredictable. It wasn't my fault. I was the victim of circumstances.

Where would I be now if I continued to think that way? Would my life have changed? No. It wouldn't.

Albert Einstein said "We cannot solve our problems with the same thinking we used when we created them"

When.... WE.... created them. Who creates the problems in your life? You. There is so much wisdom in this quote. We create our problems with our thinking, and in order to solve our problems, we need to change our thinking.

Furthermore, there is no such thing as a problem. If you have a problem, there is a problem with your thinking.

"But..." I hear you saying... "What about people who have a car accident and are paraplegic... they didn't create that problem" ... "What about people who are robbed... they didn't create that problem" ... and my answer to this is to ask you this "Which person will be better off, the one who thinks "It's not my fault my life was ruined and I'm now a cripple" or the one who thinks "I am fortunate to be alive and I will do everything in my power to live a worthwhile life"? We always have a choice on the way we think.

If you have a problem you can't solve with your current way of thinking... Change your thinking. And make sure you are in the driver's seat of your life. If you want a different life, choose who you want to be and create a different version of you.

Because you will never be any more, or any less, than you think you are.

And what you think you are, is an ever evolving thing that you can build on. The only certainty in life is that nothing is ever certain, change is inevitable... So choose how things will change for you in your life.

CHAPTER 6

DAILY TALK

Surround yourself with two kinds of people,
those who are already where you want to go,
and those who want to get where you are now.

There is a lot of truth in the saying "You can't soar with the eagles, if you are hanging with the turkeys".

Pull out your mobile phone right now and have a look at the top five people you text and call. Have a really big think about who they are and what their lives are like, because you will never be any greater than the people you associate most with. Birds of a feather really do flock together. And if you change your life, change your thoughts, change your perceptions and change your priorities, those people will either grow right along with you, or they will drop away, usually without you even having to deliberately remove them.

COACHING AND MENTORING

The higher the level of a sports person, the more likely they will have a dedicated mentor and trainer.

Olympians most certainly have a dedicated trainer... and the person that is training them will probably not be a faster runner, swimmer, jumper etc., but they will be someone who pushes them and holds them accountable.

So why would someone need a mentor to perform at their peak?

Because an ongoing conversation with someone whose sole purpose is to motivate you, ensures that your efforts are reaping the results you desire. They will assist you with setting goals, encourage you, praise you, empower you, push you and guide you.

Having positive conversations with the right people is beneficial for all of us.

Anyone, who does not encourage you, believe in you, praise you, empower you or push you - is not helpful to you. No matter how much they love you. Or how well educated they are or how long you have known them. If you want to change your life, remove the negative people. Remove the complainers and the people who allow you to complain. Remove the people who are more comfortable for you to stay how you are, not grow, not develop, and remain less than your best.

This does not mean you want people blowing hot air up your skirt saying what you want to hear. You want people around you who will tell you the truths you don't want to hear. Tell you to consider other options you have not thought of. Or tell you to pull your head in when you are being a jerk. A mentor is not a fan. A mentor is someone who helps you achieve your goals.

Surround yourself with two kinds of people:

1. People who are already where you want to go, or heading towards where you want to go, and

2. People who want to get to where you are now.

Group one will inspire you and pull you up, and if you can inspire group two and mentor them, you will gain momentum and be pushed up. Coach, and be coached. Inspire, and be inspired. Teach, and be taught.

CHAPTER 7

DAILY MANTRA

The things you hear, speak, visualise and feel ***repeatedly*** *will program your mind.*

Go back now to the 10/10 dream goals you created in our earlier chapter. The bottom part of each page where you have written your statements as though you already have the things you want can now be compiled into one document, joining together the descriptions of each section so that they all flow together. Now record yourself reading this entire text (using your phone is excellent).

Each day, play this recording to yourself, and speak along with it out loud. The more frequently you do this, and the more you focus and engage with the words you are saying, the faster you will see results.

I have been doing this on and off for several years and I can GUARANTEE if you stick to this for thirty days, you WILL see amazing results.

Remember, they must be in current tense as though you already have achieved the things you desire, be clearly explained, and in positive tense. For example, "I am slim", not "I am not fat".

The reason that this works is because you are applying the principles of brain washing (yes that is a real thing). You have designed those statements to match the life and goals you want to achieve. Every time you hear them and speak them and think them, you also imagine those images and have those feelings. With this process you are developing new neurological pathways in your brain. These pathways become stronger and stronger the more you repeat them.

As a very simple example, a person who drives a Ferrari has the supporting neurological pathways and beliefs for them to have that car. If you want that car, that relationship, that body, that job, that bank balance, those opportunities, you need to develop those same neurons in your brain to support that reality.

You literally can re-program yourself by choice to have, do and be anything you choose.

No one needs to live with the programming they currently have – or the life they currently have. Anyone can easily reprogram themselves and change their life... Including you.

BE THE PARENT OF YOUR OWN MIND

We all have tens of thousands of thoughts every day. So now you are choosing to spend some time each day re-programming your thoughts and beliefs to match the life you want. Instead of just letting life happen to you, you are making changes to your MIND so you can have, do and be the things you desire.

What about all the thoughts and beliefs that you previously had? Will they just disappear? No. You've been programmed to think a certain way for a very long time. Those neurological pathways are like super highways through your brain and they will keep firing all your old thoughts and beliefs without you even meaning to.

It is important to be mindful and pay attention to your thoughts. If you desire to be 'slim, fit, heathy, sexy and attractive' and you repeat this as part of your daily talk, take note of thoughts you have that do not support this. They are your old thoughts that need to be replaced. If you catch yourself thinking or saying 'I can't lose weight' or 'I'm unfit' or 'I have a slow metabolism' – stop yourself. Say "Cancel that" and then speak or think your new empowering belief.

RECOGNISE the thought, Stop and CANCEL it, then REPLACE it with the new thought – I have, I am, I can.

Be especially diligent in counteracting limiting beliefs that have been graced upon you by other people such as Doctors, Teachers and other authorities. These professionals have our trust, so often we blindly accept their opinions without questioning any alternatives. You don't have to live with the limitations other people have placed upon you.

You can be slim and healthy even if your current state is overweight with diabetes.

You can become smart and educated even if you have been told you have a 'learning disability'.

The world is full of people who have achieved things they were told they couldn't.

You can have, do and be anything you can believe you can. Change your beliefs and you will change your life.

CHAPTER 8

WHAT ARE YOU BUYING IN TO?

Question your beliefs... Again, question your beliefs.

A belief is something that you've been presented with, and become sold on. Someone, somewhere, at some time, has pitched an idea to you, and you have bought it. You may not even realise you bought these ideas and adapted them into your belief system. Particularly if they are beliefs that were presented to you when you were just a child. Life does that to you... tricks you with its sneaky little mind mapping. Maybe you even sold a belief to yourself, after you had an experience of some kind. Either way, what you believe, is what you've bought into... you are invested. Beliefs can be tough to change – even irrational ones!

Here is an example.

You lock your house because you believe that will protect you and keep you and your possessions safe.

If you got to work, and realised you hadn't locked the back door, you may even feel quite worried about it.

Because you *believe* that it is the locked door that prevents invasion.

What would happen if you really were in a home invasion?

What if the front and back door were both dead locked, and you heard someone trying to get in?

What if the intruder was able to crow-bar the security door, and the solid door right off the frame quicker than you could get to your phone or unlock the alternate exit door and escape?

This situation happened to me. Do you think my beliefs changed? I was most certainly sold on a new belief. My new belief was that if someone has the intention to break in to your house, they will do so, and by locking your house like fort Knox, you are preventing your own exit. I didn't lock my house after that for over fifteen years... and you know what? Nothing was ever stolen.

The point of that story was not about locking your house. The point of that story was this: Question your beliefs... Again: Question your beliefs. Don't just 'buy' what everyone else is buying. The world is full of sheep, don't be one.

Beliefs are an important part of the framework of your life. Most of what you believe has been sold to you as a buy-one-get-one-free package deal that got handed down to you by your parents.

What if some of the things you believe were actually limiting you from having the things you want? Which, in fact, you already know they are because you already learned that in a previous chapter.

These beliefs are called "Limiting Beliefs".

Exercise

Do this slowly and give yourself time to think.

Think of something you would really love to do, but haven't.

Have other people like you done this before?

Now ask yourself why you haven't you done this thing that you would like to do?

Whatever the answers were to the second question, those are your limiting beliefs.

Now ask yourself, what would I have to believe instead, to do this thing I want?

This is an exercise to open up your mind and question your beliefs. Which leads us to the next questions.

Is my limiting belief serving me in achieving my goals?

What will happen if I keep believing this?

What won't happen if I keep believing this?

What else could I choose to believe instead?

By asking yourself questions, you are opening up your mind to seek different answers to the ones you have been programmed to assume.

Use this exercise to understand which beliefs you want to change – then include those 'new beliefs' in your daily mantra.

CHAPTER 9

YOU HAVE TO FLAP TO FLY

Great change happens when very small actions are REPEATED.

This is possibly the most important principle of progress. If you take just one thing from this book, it would be that great change happens from very small actions, which are REPEATED.

No bird ever flew by hoping. No bird ever flew by praying.

In order to fly, a bird has to flap, pushing the air down, and its body up. The repetitive motion, once learned, becomes easy.

And so it is for any type of upward progression.

Faithful

Long term

Applied

Persistence

In order to move against gravity, you must create a force which will propel you upwards by your repeated actions. Small actions - REPEATED create enormous RESULTS.

You've heard the saying "sh*t rolls downhill"?

Well, this is the one time you shouldn't 'go with the flow'.

There's no glory in hanging with the turkeys - because turkeys don't fly!

If you want to be great, you must be committed to repeatedly flapping your upward drive, whatever that may be in your instance.

That may be the extra shift you do at work to save for a house, or the course you enrol in to learn a new skill. It may be as simple as taking a pill, or the commitment to weekly fitness training, the daily mantra you chant in the car on the way to work, or any ongoing and repetitive action you undertake to make yourself better than you are now.

You will recognise a 'flap' action because it is:

Repetitive - Daily ritual
Achievable - Not difficult to do just once
Long Term - To have an effect it must be repeated over a duration of time
Promotes you - This can be in any area of your life - a skill, knowledge, financial position, physical state, emotional state, status or situation.
Without 'flap' you will not progress. You will not fly.

My partner and I went to the National Achievers Congress recently and listened to some of the most well respected success mentors in our country, and one of the speakers spoke about 'daily rituals' - I thought to myself "This is the flap principle". He said he had seventeen daily rituals he undertook to ensure he was always on the path of achieving his full potential - the first of which was that every morning, as he puts his feet on the floor, he says out loud "I love my life" - How simple is that? The difference that just this small, simple, daily ritual will make to a person's life is incredible.

Everybody applies the FLAP principle in order to stay alive.

All of the basic biological needs, such as eating and sleeping are flap activities. They keep us alive.

It's the flap activities that we do, over and above keeping alive that determine the quality of our lives.

Some flap activities damage our lives, like smoking, drinking, taking drugs, criticising, complaining, and eating rubbish food.

Even thoughts are flap activities. For example, if every day you think a certain thing to yourself, it will affect your life. If every day you think how crap life is, or how stupid people are, this will have a huge long term effect on your life. In contrast, if every day you think how lucky you are to be alive, or how kind people are, this will have a very different long term effect than the first set of thought 'flaps'. If one person thought the first set of thoughts daily, and another person thought the second set of thoughts daily, those two people would end up with vastly different lives in the long term.

Even a small change to your thoughts can have a great effect. If you are interested in learning more about big change through daily habits, the book "Pivot, by Adam Markel" is a worthwhile investment.

The direction of your 'flap' is the direction of your flight. Choose your daily rituals deliberately and carefully, because they have a huge impact on your life.

CHAPTER 10

LET IT GO

Until you let go, you will be like a puppet at the mercy of your past and your fears.

"Let it go, let it go, don't hold it back anymore..."

Whether it is an emotion, an object, or a person – clutch on to nothing. Let go and have faith that what is meant for you, will be there for you. Life becomes infinitely easier when you let go.

Some people are like Velcro, they attach feeling to everything and let nothing go, this can apply to objects, situations or people. Life becomes hard if you are hooking on to everything.

EMOTIONAL 'STUFF'

We all have 'things' in our past that hurt. Things that have happened that were unfair, things that frightened us or destroyed a piece of us. People that let us down or betrayed us, hopes that were shattered, things that were denied to us, taken from us. Fears or insecurities. Situations and people that angered us so much that our very souls burned like fire.

Some people's stories are so filled with these 'things' that it tears my heart to just hear them, let alone having to endure them.

The week before my lungs collapsed and I was rushed to hospital to be diagnosed with Cancer I attended my one and only Psychologist appointment with the intention of seeking support with my relationship breakdown.

The psychologist explained to me that every piece of information we are exposed to in our lives, we mentally and emotionally 'label and file' neatly. This ensures that our mind is able to process the information, and access it easily. We develop our 'labelling and filing' system as we grow up. The more comprehensive your filing system, the more equipped you are to handle life.

When we receive information that we cannot 'label and file' it remains 'unresolved' and we will leave it out on our mental and emotional desk space (or even worse, stuff it down in a deep desk drawer). Our desk space clutters up with unfiled events and information, and this 'mess' is what makes up what is commonly referred to as our 'baggage'.

She also explained that when we are exposed to a situation that does not align with our filing systems' beliefs and values, we will either need to adjust our system to accommodate the new conflicting information, or remove ourselves from it (reject it) – as exposure to things our minds cannot accept is uncomfortable.

A simple example of this is homophobia. If a person's mental filing system has 'man + woman = acceptable' without any alternate accepted 'filing system'. Then being exposed to 'man + man' will cause discomfort, requiring either a 'new accepted filing category' or a complete removal and rejection.

Where there is direct conflict with a situation and how it should be filed, for example someone we love and trust betrays us or does something bad to us, we have extreme difficulty reconciling how to 'file' that information. Often we choose to ignore the bad thing, or reject the person.

Whatever the circumstance, things that have not been 'filed' are still unresolved. It is easy to identify these things because when you think of them, the emotions are still present and can still hurt and damage you.

These are the things that hold us back. These are the things that 'trigger' poor strategies and responses when new present day situations arise. These are the things that trigger our fear and fight or flight response. These things cause us problems in our current life and conflict in our relationships. Even phobias fall into the category of emotional baggage.

The more 'stuff' you can let go of, the easier your life will become. Letting go doesn't mean forgetting or pretending things didn't happen. Letting go means being able to process and file the events so that the real time emotion is no longer chaining you down and holding you back in your life moving forward.

Often people will go and see a counsellor or psychologist when they feel their emotional or mental baggage is interrupting their ability to enjoy life. This may help some people who need to talk through issues or sort out strategies for healthier thought processes or communication, however I have seen people spend literally years in counselling with only minimal progress.

During my studies with 'The Life Coaching College' I was privileged to learn Neuro Linguistic Programming (NLP) and time line therapy. There are many powerful tools available to unload baggage, emotions, and release the past WITHOUT having to talk about it. In fact, talking about problems, especially repeatedly, over long periods of time, can be considered damaging as you are repeating again and again the 'story' of your negative situation, and this enforces those images, those emotions, those associations and beliefs, in your mind.

I have personally witnessed Anthony Robbins do a time line exercise in a room of three thousand people. The entire room over a period of thirty minutes, first sat in darkened silence as he spoke, then gradually the room was filled with people crying and wailing, and within another ten minutes, he had guided them back into a state of victorious triumph as they had personal breakthrough. People walk out changed.

I appreciate that if you have never been exposed to NLP or Anthony Robbins this may seem quite bizarre and even frightening. I have to confess that my partner and I stepped outside as it was just too much emotion for us in one room. However the exercises when done one-on-one with a trained NLP Master Practitioner are powerful and liberating and are the quickest and easiest way I have found to resolve emotional 'stuff'. Anger, fear, sadness, guilt – all can be melted away so that they no longer come up in day-to-day life.

Negative people can be collapsed, parental scarring resolved and traumatic situations turned as dull as a stale biscuit. One of Anthony Robbins quotes is "It's never too late to have a happy childhood" and after learning NLP I finally understood how that could be possible for all people regardless of their history.

If you can identify any recurring emotions such as anger, fear, jealousy, guilt, sadness, or you know there are things you need to let go of, seek a qualified and experienced NLP Practitioner's assistance, and make sure it is someone you feel comfortable with.

When you let go, life becomes easier, and you are better equipped to respond to life. This will make space for you to receive many positive things in your life that may have previously eluded you. Imagine how free you will feel without clutter, stresses and worries on your mind.

CHAPTER 11

SHARING & CARING

It is in giving that we truly receive.

I was one of those kids that just completely missed the point of schooling. I knew all kids had to go there, but the point of it just by-passed me at the time. If I could go back now I would be the most diligent, studious and devoted child, but at the time with my limited understanding of life, studying wasn't a priority.

Thankfully I was bright and a quick learner, so I actually did learn, in spite of my lack of effort.

Exam days would come, and all the other kids would be there before school, studying their piles of notes, reading their books, trying to get the best marks they could and to be helpful, I would offer to ask them questions to help them study. I could see they were stressed. They were saying they might fail, that they hadn't studied enough. They were panicking. So I would say, 'I'll help you'. I couldn't understand why they thought a high school exam was so important, after all, what was the worst thing that could happen?

So I would go through the revision with them.

What is the symbol for Iron on the periodic table?

What colour does litmus paper turn if a solution is acidic?

Name the parts of a cell?

I wasn't interested in studying, I was interested in HELPING. But when I went into the exams, I would come out with high marks.

Because it is impossible to help someone else, without gaining something even greater for yourself.

There is no exception to this rule, and I will tell you why.

No matter what stage you are at in life... living in the street or living in a palace. You always have the opportunity to help someone in some way. Helping others will change the way you perceive yourself, will change your opportunities, will change your level of happiness, will develop you, grow you, and edify you.

If you meet someone that says "I'm not interested in helping strangers, I've got enough problems of my own" pity them, because they have not yet understood what greatness is, and success will elude them, they might get a taste of it, but they will be forever chasing something they cannot quite achieve, looking for recognition for their accomplishments, and living with the niggling feeling of wanting more, because they will never be satisfied. Satisfaction aka 'happiness' really does come from giving, far more than receiving.

CHAPTER 12

YOU ARE WHAT YOU EAT

Mental health, emotional health and physical health are inter-related.

This old cliché doesn't just apply to your body. It is also true for your emotional and mental state.

Your feelings are caused by chemicals in your brain. The chemicals in your brain are reliant on nutrients.

Our bodies are made up of complex systems which rely on many different processes. These processes cannot happen without the ingredients required for operation.

Aside from the obvious things like making blood cells, building strong bones, developing muscle tissue – your body releases and synthesises a whole stack of goodies that keep you feeling calm, happy, energetic and motivated.

If you are not feeling calm, happy, energetic and motivated – your brain is lacking in the chemicals needed for these feelings.

You may be feeling stressed, anxious or depressed due to certain other chemicals being released in your body. The ones related to survival.

Changing your lifestyle to include a healthy balanced diet is the first step to physical, emotional and mental health, however due to other factors such as malabsorption, hereditary deficiencies, processing of foods, and certain farming practices it is still possible to be malnourished while eating well.

My personal view is that supplementation is advisable, particularly if you are experiencing any physical, mental or emotional symptoms. For advice about supplementation, a Nutritional Therapist is trained to identify and treat nutrition based symptoms.

It is also advisable to avoid sugar. It plays havoc with your system and your hormones and supplies no nutritional value.

My partner and I take up to twenty supplements on alternate days. We enjoy fresh vegetables, fruits, nuts, seeds and natural proteins daily and avoid processed grains and sugars. We cook a vegetable and protein breakfast daily and prepare most meals from scratch without packets and prepared foods. I avoid processed meats such as sausages, premade rissoles and lunch meats. We eat natural fats, butter, coconut oil, cold pressed olive oil not processed margarine and vegetable oils. I avoid anything that says 'sugar free', 'lite', 'diet', 'low fat' as that typically means lots of added 'chemicals'.

The impact on wellbeing is noticeable. The impact on youthful appearance is noticeable. Eating well and ensuring your body has all the nutrients it needs is critical to feeling good, looking good and feeling happy.

SUMMARY – THE 'HOW TO' IN SIMPLE TERMS

1. Assess where you are right now in the eight areas of your life.

2. Create in words a picture of the 'ideal' feelings and circumstances as positive statements for each of the eight areas using "I am" and "I have" and "I can" statements. These are your detailed life goals written as though you have already achieved them.

3. Record these as one continuous recording on your phone and listen and repeat them out loud daily, really picturing and feeling these as reality.

4. Be aware of your feelings and own them. When you feel worried, upset, frustrated, and angry – ask yourself "What about this situation is triggering this feeling? What am I thinking that is causing this feeling? What do I believe that is causing this feeling?" Consciously choose another belief / thought and recognise that all feelings come from within us from our own thoughts. Own your emotions. Believe good things and use faith as a defence against doubt and fear.

5. Design in your mind the image of the 'ideal you' and spend a few minutes each day just focusing on this version of you in your mind and how great you feel being this happy, confident, successful, fit, healthy version of yourself. The optimum you.

6. Police your thoughts – Recognise, Cancel and Replace those that don't support your goals.

7. Challenge your limiting beliefs and replace them with empowering beliefs.

8. Thank, thank, thank. Every day – Spend time being grateful. If you have no job, be grateful for your vision, your mind and your health. If you have no legs, be grateful for your arms, your parents and your voice. Be thankful for sunshine, for public transport, for the food on your plate.

9. Find someone who has the life you want, and model them. If you can surround yourself with people who inspire you, motivate you, and encourage you. Remove toxic people from your life. Bless them and let them go.

10. Be diligent in applying these principles every day. You will only change your life by changing your daily habits.

11. Clear any 'baggage' you may unknowingly be carrying around by seeking assistance from a qualified and experienced NLP Practitioner.

12. Make a conscious effort to help others. This may be in the form of donating to a charity (money or time). Helping someone achieve a goal they have. Offering to teach someone something. Be dedicated to the concept of giving.

13. Use Discerning Judgment in your own life, not Critical Judgement of others.

14. Take supplements, it is estimated that up to 80% of people in first world countries are deficient in critical vitamins and minerals. Deficiencies are linked to depression, anxiety, insomnia, restlessness, fatigue and many other physical illnesses. At the very minimum take a good multivitamin each day and eat a natural, balanced diet with as little sugar as possible. If you have any health issues whatsoever, consider making an appointment with a good Nutritional Therapist.

Closing quote: "If you want your story to be magnificent, begin by realising you are the author, and every day is a new page" *Mark Houlahan*

Now go out into the world and become the most amazing version of yourself you can imagine. Live with passion and conviction – the passion and conviction that you choose and create.

RECOMMENDATIONS AND RESOURCES

Australia

www.thelifecoachingcollege.com.au – Glenn Murdoch and his team will be able to connect you with a qualified life coach and NLP Practitioner.

Pivot – Book by Adam Markel – Recommended Read.

Hay House Publishers – Buy this book and other Personal Development titles online through the publisher.

http://www.australiannaturaltherapistsassociation.com.au – Find a Nutritional Therapist

Follow us on FaceBook www.facebook.com/ NaomiStockman1108

Printed in the United States
By Bookmasters